# Cary and Randy

*Also by C.D. Payne*

Youth in Revolt: The Journals of Nick Twisp

Revolting Youth: The Further Journals of Nick Twisp

Young and Revolting: The Continental
Journals of Nick Twisp

Revoltingly Youth: The Journals of
Nick Twisp's Younger Brother

Son of Youth in Revolt: The Journals of Scott Twisp

Revolt at the Beach: More Twisp Family Chronicles

The Unpleasant Poet

Miracle in a Can

Cheeky Swimsuits of 1957

Helen of Pepper Pike

Brenda the Great

Invisibly Yours

Cut to the Twisp

Frisco Pigeon Mambo

Civic Beauties

Queen of America [play]

# Cary and Randy

a full-length biographical
play in two acts

**C.D. Payne**

Aivia Press

Copyright © 2017 by C.D. Payne
All rights reserved

CAUTION: Professionals and amateurs are hereby warned that CARY AND RANDY is subject to a royalty. It is fully protected under the copyright laws of the United States of America, and of all countries covered by the International Copyright Union (including the Dominion of Canada and the rest of the British Commonwealth), and of all countries covered by the Pan-American Copyright Convention and the Universal Copyright Convention, and of all countries with which the United States has reciprocal copyright relations. All rights, including professional, amateur, motion picture, recitation, lecturing, public reading, radio broadcast, television, e-transmission, online use, and the rights of translation into foreign languages, are strictly reserved, permission for which must be secured from the author's agent in writing. All inquiries concerning rights, professional or amateur, should be addressed to Aivia Press at apeditor@nicktwisp.com.

ISBN-13: 978-1882647217
ISBN-10: 1882647211

## Cast of characters

CARY GRANT: Film star, 38 years old (and older)

RANDOLPH SCOTT: Film star, 44 years old (and older)

WILL GRADOWSKI: 21 years old, U.S. marine (also Los Angeles cop)

The following parts can be played by as few as two actors:

VIRGINIA CHERRILL: 26 years old, film actress

PHYLLIS BROOKS: 28 years old, film actress

LOUELLA PARSONS: 62 years old, gossip columnist

ELSIE LEACH: 63 years old, Cary Grant's mother

MAE WEST: 50 years old, film actress

HARRY COHN: 52 years old, studio boss

BETSY DRAKE: 39 years old, film actress

A FILM FAN: Late 20s in party dress

Off-stage male voices: radio announcer, lawyer

# CARY AND RANDY

**Place**
Beach house at Santa Monica, CA

**Time**
Winter and Spring, 1943 and Summer, 1962

**Set requirements:** single set, interior

**Setting:** a Santa Monica beach-house living room in early evening, January, 1943. Furnishings are comfortable, but not ostentatious. Entry door is at stage right. Behind that is a hallway leading off to unseen bedrooms. On the rear wall are French doors leading to a patio. Distant surf can be heard whenever the French doors are opened. Furnishings in the room include a bookcase/bar, radio console, sofa, stuffed chair, floor lamp, coffee table, coat rack, wall mirror, and spinet piano. On stage left is a dark area that will be illuminated occasionally in the course of the action.

## ACT I
## Scene 1

At Rise: 44-year-old Randolph Scott, seated in the stuffed chair, is reading the *Wall Street Journal*. The radio is tuned to dance band music. The song ends.

RADIO ANNOUNCER (o.s.)
From NBC Radio City at Sunset and Vine in Hollywood here are tonight's news headlines. Singer Bing Crosby's Tolucca Lake home has been destroyed by fire. The popular film and radio star, who was golfing when the fire started, told reporters he felt fortunate that his wife and four sons escaped injury. Fire officials say the blaze, which gutted the 20-room

## CARY AND RANDY

mansion, was believed to have been started by a Christmas tree. In war news, the U.S. Navy has revealed the names of 10 ships lost in the Battle of the Santa Cruz Islands. These include the aircraft carrier U.S.S. Hornet, which was sunk by kamikaze attackers. Also named were three battle cruisers and seven destroyers. Meanwhile, Soviet troops have launched an all-out offensive on German forces dug in around Stalingrad. In Washington, President Roosevelt told Congress that new sacrifices and $16 billion in new taxes or "compulsory loans" would be needed to meet spending needs of $100 billion for the war effort. And now, friends, the makers of Duz detergent remind you that household drudgery can be a thing of the past when you . . .

Randolph gets up and switches off the radio as 38-year-old Cary Grant enters via the exterior door.

RANDY
Hey, there's my favorite movie star.

CARY
(looking around as he
hangs up his topcoat)
Who? Gabby Hayes? Franklin Pangborn? Marie Dressler?

RANDY
No, Archie Leach.

CARY
Oh, him.

Cary stops by a mirror and examines his face closely.

RANDY
See something fascinating in there?

## CARY AND RANDY

CARY
(still looking at himself)
I need to check how my wretched life is ruining my looks.

RANDY
Hard day at the studio?

CARY
The worst. They may change the name of the picture to "Mr. Lucky."

RANDY
"Mr. Lucky." That's not bad. It's better than "Mr. Stalled in Front of the Mirror."

CARY
I can see the reviews now. "Mr. Lucky" is just ducky. Or "Mr. Lucky" is profoundly yucky.

RANDY
What's got you in such a foul mood?

CARY
(still looking in the mirror)
Female trouble. What else?

RANDY
Your time of the month?

CARY
My wife. I need a drink. You want one?

RANDY
(pointing to table beside his chair)
Got one already.

## CARY AND RANDY

Cary tears himself away from the mirror and mixes a cocktail at the bar, as Randy returns to his paper.

CARY
Why don't they warn fellows about marriage? Getting married is like jumping naked into a pit of vipers. I'm thinking now I should have stuck it out with my first wife.

RANDY
As I recall, she wasn't planning on renewing your option.

Stage left is illuminated and we see 26-year-old Virginia Cherrill seated on the witness stand; she is being interrogated by a male lawyer (o.s.).

LAWYER'S VOICE (o.s.)
State your name, please.

VIRGINIA
Virginia Cherrill.

LAWYER'S VOICE (o.s.)
What is your occupation?

VIRGINIA
I'm a movie actress.

LAWYER'S VOICE (o.s.)
And what films might we have seen you in?

VIRGINIA
I played the blind flower girl in Charlie Chaplin's picture "City Lights." I played the sister of a racketeer in "What Price Crime."

## CARY AND RANDY

CARY
She also starred in a picture called "Money Mad." I guess that one slipped her mind!

LAWYER'S VOICE (o.s.)
How long did you cohabitate with Cary Grant as his wife?

VIRGINIA
For seven horrible, nightmarish months.

CARY
I object. It wasn't all bad, Virginia.

They take no notice of him.

LAWYER'S VOICE (o.s.)
Where did you live?

VIRGINIA
In Cary's house on West Live Oak Drive in the Los Feliz district of Los Angeles.

LAWYER'S VOICE (o.s.)
Just the two of you?

VIRGINIA
No, the actor Randolph Scott also resided there too. He was in no hurry to move out either.

RANDY
Hey, it was a big house. And I chipped in for my share of the expenses. Besides, you know what they say.

VIRGINIA
What's that?

## CARY AND RANDY

RANDY
Marriage is a three-way street.

LAWYER'S VOICE (o.s.)
Tell the court how you were treated by your new husband.

VIRGINIA
Right from the beginning Cary was very controlling and jealous. I couldn't even look at another man or he would become enraged. He had me followed by detectives. I wasn't doing anything! I never gave him any cause to be suspicious. Of course, a person in my position has to dress well. He got very nasty if I bought so much as a pair of stockings. I could barely pry a dollar out of him for groceries. He ridiculed my acting as well. He was always running me down any way he could.

LAWYER'S VOICE (o.s.)
And was your husband loving toward you?

VIRGINIA
Hardly. The man was a cold fish. It was all I could do to get him to touch me.

LAWYER'S VOICE (o.s.)
And did your husband abuse alcohol?

VIRGINIA
He did. He drank to excess, and that would scare me. Because then he became violent. He choked and kicked me. He beat me and threatened to kill me.

LAWYER'S VOICE (o.s.)
Mr. Grant beat you with his fists?

## CARY AND RANDY

**CARY**
Objection! That's leading the witness.

**LAWYER'S VOICE (o.s.)**
You allege that your husband was violent toward you?

**VIRGINIA**
Yes, he was. On numerous occasions. He struck me and I got blood all over my clothes.

**LAWYER'S VOICE (o.s.)**
And what would your husband say later when you remonstrated with him for these brutal attacks?

**VIRGINIA**
He acted like he didn't know what I was talking about. He would say I must have fallen on my own and hurt myself. It was like he blotted everything out of his memory. I began to think he must be crazy or deranged. After seven months of hell, I couldn't take it any more. I had to leave him because I feared for my life.*

Stage left goes dark.

**CARY**
Well, that's her side of the story. OK, I wasn't an ideal husband. But hell, it was my first time being married. You can't expect perfection the first time out. If living with women was easy, 10,000 divorce lawyers would be starving as we speak.

**RANDY**
Plus, you married an actress. They're known to be trouble.

---
*Ms. Cherrill's statements are based on divorce court testimony as reported by the *Los Angeles Times*.

## CARY AND RANDY

CARY

I know. Annoying as hell on set and then the director expects you to kiss them like you mean it. Half the time their breath would gag a goat. Anyway, Virginia neglected to mention that we're good friends now. We get together whenever she's in town. I took her dancing at the Trocadero a few months ago. We had a great time.

RANDY

Yeah, I know. I was there.

CARY

I need another drink. You ready for a refill?

RANDY
(handing him his glass).

Sure.

CARY

You should have talked me out of marrying that girl.

RANDY

I make a point never to interfere when a fellow's digging his own grave. And yours seemed like an especially deep pit.

CARY

I loved her, you know. She was the first girl I ever loved. I thought we'd be together forever.

RANDY

Right.

CARY

I suppose you thought it was doomed from the beginning?

**CARY AND RANDY**

RANDY

Well, I didn't quite understand why you had to sneak off to England to marry her.

CARY

It was just how things worked out. I didn't mean to offend anyone.

Cary hands Randy his freshened drink.

RANDY

Here's to better days.

They clink glasses.

RANDY

Are you spending the night?

CARY

I thought I might. Do you mind?

RANDY

Not at all. Your name's still on the deed. Hungry?

CARY

No, I'm fine. How about you?

RANDY

I ate earlier. Want to call up someone and go out on the town?

CARY

Ah, let's stay in and make a night of it. I may have a guest showing up later.

## CARY AND RANDY

RANDY

Oh? Anyone I know?

CARY

A young marine I met who may be shipping out soon.

RANDY

Doing your bit for the war effort, huh?

CARY

We have to keep up the morale of the troops. I hope you don't mind.

RANDY

You know me. I'm easy. Bette Davis opened the Hollywood Canteen. And now Cary Grant opens up his home.

CARY

It sounds like you do mind. You know I like a bit of variety in the bedroom.

RANDY

We could change the wallpaper and the drapes. Just pulling your leg, partner. I'm not the jealous type.

CARY

That's so refreshing. Why can't wives have that attitude? How is my having a spot of fun hurting her? Anyway I'm not calling Barbara. She knows where to find me if she wants me.

RANDY

I'm sure she does.

CARY

You know, the girl I should have married was Phyllis Brooks.

**CARY AND RANDY**

I had the chance too. I thought I was done with love and then Brooksie came into my life. Remember how much fun she was?

RANDY

Of course. Don't forget she and I were in that Shirley Temple picture together.

CARY

Right! "Rebecca of Sunnybrook Farm." Little Shirley stole the show as usual. I'm told that adorable minx has a crush on me.

RANDY

Everyone has a crush on you, including Cary Grant.

CARY

Well, that's not true. I can hardly stand the man. I'm Archie Leach, the son of a poor pants presser from Bristol, England. Every day I have to walk around disguised as Cary Grant, the distinguished film star and debonair man about town. It's a big burden.

RANDY

You don't have to be Cary Grant around me.

CARY

Oh? Who should I be then?

RANDY

Just be yourself.

CARY

The last time I tried that I was walking around on stilts at Coney Island for eight bucks a day. And was lucky to get that

## CARY AND RANDY

job. Damn! Why didn't I marry Phyllis Brooks when I had the chance?

RANDY
As I recall there were complications.

Stage left illuminates, revealing 28-year-old Phyllis Brooks.

PHYLLIS
Sure, I loved Cary Grant. God knows I still love the man. I probably always will. I wanted to marry him too. We talked about it. He even gave me a ring. Then he went running to his lawyers. He had them draw up a contract he wanted me to sign. A multi-page thing full of sleazy legalese. It stated that if the marriage didn't work out we would make no financial claims on each other. It was like he was expecting our marriage to fail even before it began. That was bad enough. He also stipulated in the contract that I was never to invite my mother over to our house. Can you imagine that? He had the nerve to put it in writing that my mother was to be excluded from our lives!

CARY
No one would blame me if they met her mother. What a dragon! Phyllis was lucky I didn't insist that witch never set foot on the same continent as us.

PHYLLIS
I admit my mother didn't like Cary. She wasn't disguising it much either. She was just trying to protect me. She was aware of the rumors about him. I was too, of course. But people can be vicious about movie stars. Everyone knows that. My mother heard how Cary treated his first wife and didn't want me to have to go through anything like that. But Cary always assured me that he had changed.

## CARY AND RANDY

CARY
I did! I had!


PHYLLIS
Anyway, I refused to sign that contract. After that, we sort of drifted apart. Then I heard he'd taken up with Barbara Hutton, the richest woman in the world. Cary was always tight with a dollar, so I could see how he'd be attracted to that mountain of cash. Barbara sounded to me like she could be a handful, but I always wished them the best.

Stage left goes dark.

CARY
Women are so damn complicated. And scheming. And demanding. Plus they're always dragging in their mothers to give you hell. Now I know why I avoided them all those years.

RANDY
That would be when you were living in New York with that dress designer?

CARY
Jack Kelly mostly designed costumes. And never mind him. At least that's one thing I don't have to worry about with Barbara. Her mother's dead.

RANDY
Suicide, wasn't it?

CARY
When Barbara was six. She was the one who discovered the body.

## CARY AND RANDY

RANDY

That's a tough break.

CARY

My childhood was just as grim. At least she always got enough to eat.

Cary again examines his face in the wall mirror.

RANDY

Something amiss, Miss Grant?

CARY

Just me. I'm looking so goddam old!

RANDY

You're six years younger than me.

CARY

That's fine for you, Randy. People expect those yodeling stars of westerns to be grizzled.

RANDY

I don't yodel. It's right there in my contract. I don't play the guitar either. Hell, I don't even whistle.
(chuckling)
That reminds me. I got waylaid by a reporter from one of those fan magazines today. She asked me about my philosophy of acting.

CARY

Your what?

RANDY

My philosophy of acting. Like I was another John Barrymore.

## CARY AND RANDY

I got very serious and told her my approach to acting was to try not to fall off the horse.

Cary doesn't laugh at the jest; he continues to scrutinize his face in the mirror.

                    CARY

You say things like that, Randy, because you don't take your career seriously.

                    RANDY

Sure I do. All the way to the bank.

Cary pinches the skin under his chin.

                    CARY

I'm getting a goddam double chin. Look at that. Next thing you know I'll be competing with Sidney Greenstreet for fat-guy roles.

A photo of Sidney Greenstreet is projected on a scrim at stage left.

                    RANDY

Not likely. I think your main competition would be Cuddles Sakall.

A photo of the character actor S.Z. "Cuddles" Sakall is projected on the scrim.

                    CARY

Thanks a lot!

                    RANDY

Just go easy on the booze, porky. That's what packs on the pounds.

### CARY AND RANDY

#### CARY
Easy for you to say. You're not married to my wife. Shall I freshen your drink?

#### RANDY
Why, Mr. Grant, I believe you're trying to get me intoxicated!

#### CARY
I'm taking that as a yes.

Cary collects the glasses and returns to the bar.

#### RANDY
Speaking of getting older, our birthdays are next week.

#### CARY
I know. I love that you were born in the same century as Charles Dickens, Abraham Lincoln, and Queen Victoria. Whereas I was born in the same century as Mickey Rooney, Baby Leroy, and the Dionne quintuplets. I suppose you'll want to have a party.

#### RANDY
Why not? We could have it here. I could hire a bartender and maybe get a small jazz band. Have some music and dancing. Serve a buffet supper at midnight. Then blow out the candles. How's that sound?

#### CARY
It sounds OK. But I'm not inviting my wife. No fun for poor Archie if she's here. She'll either offend my friends or feel like she's been insulted. And I know she'll insist on leaving early. But I can't come without a date. Who should I ask?

## CARY AND RANDY

**RANDY**

You could come with me.

**CARY**

That's sweet, but I can't dance with you. You're a fellow. What would people think?

**RANDY**

It was just a thought. I'm sure Cary Grant can get a date if he puts his mind to it.

**CARY**

I should pick someone who will cause Barbara maximum annoyance.

**RANDY**

I think I win in that category too.

**CARY**

I'm serious, Randy. You know how insecure Barbara is. I need to show her I can't be led around by the nose like some trained monkey. That's the trouble with wives: they're always interfering in your life.

Cary hands Randy his refilled glass.

**RANDY**

Here's to a memorable party.

They clink glasses.

**CARY**

If we have to get old and decrepit, let's do it in style.

**RANDY**

Always.

## CARY AND RANDY

Cary sits at the piano bench and taps out a sad tune with one finger.

**CARY**
Hey, you took down our Christmas tree.

**RANDY**
It was time. The thing was a fire hazard.

**CARY**
You should call up Bing Crosby and suggest he do the same.

**RANDY**
I hear it's a bit late for that now.

Cary takes a gulp of his drink and sets it back on the piano. He plays a familiar tune.

**CARY** (singing)
I met my million-dollar nightmare at a five and ten cents store. That's not quite right. Let's try this: I met my million-dollar ex-wife at a five and ten cents store. That sounds about right.

**RANDY**
So what's your problem now with Barbara?

**CARY**
Do you have any idea what I face when I go home?

**RANDY**
No, tell me.

**CARY**
OK, I'm tired. I've had a long, grueling day at the studio.

## CARY AND RANDY

Idiot directors are telling me how to act, costume designers are dressing me like a rube from the sticks, and producers are making snide comments loud enough for me to overhear. So I go home. I walk in the door and I'm facing two dozen of her ritzy friends. Every night it's the same story. The woman can't eat a meal unless it's a big-budget Technicolor production with a full cast of extras. And she expects me to be the star. Hell, half the twits at the table are conversing in French. And every time I turn around I'm bumping into another servant. She's got a secretary, a paid companion, a valet, a chauffeur, a cook, and more maids than the Queen of Sheba. Most of them speaking French too. Last time I counted we had 30 servants. And all eating on our dime. It's like living in a zoo!

RANDY
Well, you did marry the heiress to the Woolworth's fortune. That's a tall stack of nickels and dimes. You can't expect her to live in a hut on the beach.

CARY
You should talk, Randy. You were married to a du Pont. They make gunpowder, a very lucrative business. People love to blow stuff up. Those du Ponts are richer than all the Warner brothers put together.

RANDY
True. But I was smart enough to keep Marion safely stashed away at her horse farm in Virginia. I hardly ever saw the woman.

CARY
Probably a good thing too, since she was old enough to be your mother. Why did you marry her, anyway?

## CARY AND RANDY

RANDY

All the Vanderbilts were taken.

CARY

So how was she in the sack?

RANDY
(southern accent)

Sir, a gentleman from the South never discusses such matters.

CARY

Did you actually sleep with her?

RANDY

Let's leave Marion out of this discussion. She's a good friend of mine. I like her a lot despite once having been married to her.

CARY

Do you like her more than you like me?

RANDY

I like you, Marion du Pont, Laurel and Hardy, and Lassie. But I like my horse best of all.

CARY

I thought so. At least you made out well in the divorce settlement. My first marriage was a financial disaster. Hey, this is not cheering me up. What's new with you?

RANDY

I had lunch with Joel today. He thinks L.A. is going to boom big-time after the war. He's buying orange groves and horse ranches in the San Fernando Valley. He thinks they're a good investment.

## CARY AND RANDY

CARY

That would be Joel McCrea, the exceedingly handsome and virile movie star?

A photo of bare-chested Joel McCrea is projected on the scrim.

RANDY

That's the one. Did you know a woman once fainted right on this beach from the sight of Joel McCrea in a bathing suit? Her eyes fluttered up and *bang*, she keeled right over on the sand.

CARY

What press agent dreamed up that story?

RANDY

No, it's true. Joel confirmed it. He was terribly embarrassed by the whole thing.

CARY

He was, huh? Sounds like you two have been getting rather cozy.

RANDY

Not likely. He's got a pretty wife in his ranch house and he's not sneaking out to the bunkhouse for any romps.

CARY

You need to take a break from those westerns, Tex. I think you've got sagebrush poisoning. Land, huh? I'd rather own a well-managed office building on Wilshire. Or an attractive little oil well. Too many headaches trying to develop land.

## CARY AND RANDY

RANDY

Well, good luck finding one of those at a decent price. Course your portfolio's pretty stuffed now with dime stores.

CARY

Funny, I used to shop at Woolworth's back in Bristol--the few times I had a sixpence in my pocket. Now I wouldn't be caught dead in one.

RANDY

You don't go in to count the receipts? Wait on a few customers at the lunch counter?

CARY

You're the one whose family was big in commerce, pal. If any of us poor Leaches had ever scraped up enough coppers to get on a boat to America, I might have wound up cleaning the toilets in one of your textile factories. For 19 cents an hour.

RANDY

I doubt we'd pay you that much. But I might be keeping my eye on you right now for possible advancement.

CARY

No doubt. You'd have me polishing your car--among other things.

A doorbell rings.

CARY

That may be my young marine. You'll be nice to him, Randy?

RANDY

I'll be pleasant to him. I expect you're the one who'll be nice to him.

**CARY AND RANDY**

Cary opens the exterior door.

> CARY
>
> Hello. Nice to see you. Do come in.

Will Gradowski, a handsome young marine, enters and looks around shyly.

> WILL
>
> Good evening, Mr. Grant. I, I hope I'm not intruding.

> CARY
>
> Not at all. It's lovely to see you. This is Randy Scott, a fellow I know who's trying to break into the movies.

Will grabs Randy's hand and shakes it.

> WILL
>
> I've seen all your films, Mr. Scott. I think you're the greatest. The name's Will Gradowski, but most folks call me Will.

> RANDY
>
> Nice to meet you, Will. You can call me Randy. Mr. Scott is my old man back in North Carolina.

> CARY
>
> Would you like a drink, Will? We're having Manhattans.

> WILL (nervous)
>
> Some bourbon on the rocks would do me fine, if you've got that.

> CARY
>
> Coming right up. You can hang your coat on that rack.

## CARY AND RANDY

Cary goes over to the bar as Will hangs up his coat. Cary studies his uniformed figure.

CARY
So we should address you as Corporal Gradowski?

WILL
I just got my new stripe. I was kind of shocked to get the promotion. I kind of expected to be a private the whole war. Wow, this place is sure swanky. And it's right on the beach too. I mean you can walk right outside and there's the sand and there's the Pacific ocean.

CARY
Not to mention the sunbathers, the dog-walkers, and those athletic lifeguards. Randy likes to be rescued at least twice a week.

RANDY
And we have a pool too, Will.

WILL
Wow, you have your own private swimming pool! Right next to the ocean! How about that. And you can walk up to the pier and buy a hamburger any time you want. And not even get in your car. Back home we have to drive 14 miles over bad roads to get so much as a donut.

RANDY
It's a convenient location. We like it.

CARY
It was built originally for Norma Talmadge, the silent star. She co-starred with Randy in that classic 1916 film "Going Straight."

## CARY AND RANDY

**RANDY**
Not likely. I was still in high school back then.

**WILL**
I've read all about this house. The movie magazines call it Bachelor Hall. They say there's a constant stream of beautiful starlets running in and out day and night.

**CARY**
(looking about)
Damn, Randy. Where are all the beautiful girls?

**RANDY**
Beats me, pal. They must have taken the night off.

Cary hands Will his drink.

**CARY**
Don't believe everything you read, kid.

Stage left illuminates, revealing Louella Parsons, typing away on a vintage manual typewriter.

**WILL**
Isn't that Louella Parsons, the famous gossip columnist?

**CARY**
That's her, demonstrating the surprising fact that a snake can type.

Louella stops typing and turns forward.

**LOUELLA**
Sure, I'd like to get the goods on Cary Grant. What a story that would be. I mean it's not like it's any big secret around

town. Just look at who his friends are: Noel Coward, Cole Porter, William Haines and that whole lavender crowd. Plus, he's been playing footsy with Randolph Scott forever. But libel laws being what they are you need incontrovertible proof. An arrest for indecency would be ideal.

CARY
Dream on, Louella. That's not going to happen.

LOUELLA
Hah! You think I didn't hear about that incident in the department store? A major star caught in the act in a public men's room. I got the call two minutes after they slapped on the handcuffs. But the studios have too much clout with the vice squad. They put the fix in fast.

CARY
Never happened. It was some other poor sap.

LOUELLA
Yes, the patsy they paid to take your place. But I have my small triumphs. You know how Cary Grant found out his first wife was divorcing him? He read about it in my column. I also covered Randolph Scott's bizarre marriage to that du Pont woman. I'm no innocent, but I can't even imagine what that was all about. And neither can my readers.

RANDY
Aw, go crawl back under your rock, Louella. And take Hedda Hopper with you!

LOUELLA
So who's your young friend, Cary?

## CARY AND RANDY

CARY

This is Adolph Gutenhopper, a German secret agent disguised as a United States marine. I've just passed him the blueprints of the Douglas Aircraft factory which I obtained by having an illicit affair with Judy Garland's mother.

LOUELLA

Thanks for the scoop, Cary. That will be my lead in tomorrow's column.

She returns to her typewriter.

Stage left goes dark.

WILL (anxious)

Is she really going to print that?

CARY

I hope so. When my lawyers finish with her there'll be nothing left but a small ugly stain. Have a seat, Will. Tell us about yourself.

They sit down.

WILL

I'm from Iowa. Council Bluffs. Well, outside of Council Bluffs. My folks have a farm there. 240 acres. Mostly corn and soybeans. A few cows, lots of chickens. No pigs, though, my mom can't abide the smell.

CARY

Sounds like a real cosmopolitan place. Is this your first time on the West Coast?

### CARY AND RANDY

**WILL**
It's pretty much my first time anywhere, except for our senior class trip to Washington, D.C. We took the train. We passed Eleanor Roosevelt in the White House. She smiled at us.

**CARY**
That must have been a thrill.

**RANDY**
I hear you may be shipping out soon.

**WILL**
Yeah, probably. I just finished all my training. Down at Camp Pendleton. I'm a radio corpsman.

**RANDY**
Cary does radio too.

**WILL**
I know. I heard him many times on the Lux Radio Theater. I always make a point of tuning in when they announce Mr. Grant is going to be on the show. He's my favorite actor.

**CARY**
You're very kind to say so, Will. I certainly hope dear Randy here is your second favorite.

**WILL**
Oh, he is! He is! I'd be nervous as hell being on national radio. All those millions of people out there. But you always sound so calm. And you never flub your lines either.

**RANDY**
He downs a couple of stiff drinks before he faces the microphone. Say, we ought to sell someone the idea of doing a radio show based on Bachelor Hall.

## CARY AND RANDY

### CARY

That's a thought.

(imitating a radio announcer)

Presenting another episode of Bachelor Hall, where lovely young things must defend their virtue against sex-crazed actors. Starring tonight's special guests: Miss Gracie Allen and Miss Zasu Pitts.

### WILL (laughing)

Sounds like a hit show to me. So do you use Lux soap?

### CARY

Of course. I wouldn't use anything else for my delicate under-things. And for Randy's saddle blankets.

### RANDY (winking)

Keeps 'em nice and soft.

### CARY

I like radio. I don't have to worry about my tie being crooked or my hair sticking up in back.

### RANDY

Or the lights showing off your double chin.

### CARY

That too. I stroll into the studio, read my part, and they pay me a thousand dollars. What's not to like?

### WILL

And it's good publicity for your movies.

### CARY

Good point.

## CARY AND RANDY

WILL

You were always great too. 'Course I like all your movies even more.

CARY

Thanks. I appreciate that.

WILL

I guess I might be your number-one fan, Mr. Grant. Er, naturally I wouldn't want to come between you two fellas.

CARY

Don't you worry, Will. I have a wife for that. She's trying her best. And Mr. Scott has assured me that he's not the jealous type. In fact, he's presently infatuated with Joel McCrea.

RANDY

Cary, I'm beginning to suspect this young fellow is interested in more than your autograph.

Cary waits a beat before he reacts.

CARY (suavely)

Right. Well, I imagine something like that can be arranged. You've had some experience in this area?

WILL

Sure. I have a boyfriend back home. Well, Kenny's in the navy now. I've been fooling around with fellas in the barn since I was 12.

CARY

My, my, I didn't realize that sort of thing went on back in Idaho.

## CARY AND RANDY

**WILL**

Iowa. You'd be surprised. 'Course there's not a lot to do on a farm for kicks.

**CARY**

How about among you Marines? You must get restless confined in those steamy barracks.

**WILL**

Not so much. They frown on it you know. If they catch anyone, they come down like a ton of bricks. They've sent guys to prison for years. Or worse can happen. You have to pretend you're sweet on girls or you risk someone lobbing a hand grenade into your foxhole. Kenny says things are not quite so bad in the Navy. But we marines take pride in being the toughest of the tough.

**CARY**

Well, you certainly look the part.

**WILL**

I played football in high school. Defensive end. And baseball. Shortstop mostly. I hit .327 my senior year.

**CARY**

That's impressive. Can I get you another drink, Will?

**WILL**

No, thanks. One does me fine. I don't want to get too impaired. I expect I'll remember this night for the rest of my life.

**RANDY**

Cary, why don't you show our guest the rest of the house?

## CARY AND RANDY

### CARY

Be happy to. But please excuse me for a moment. I'll be right back.

Cary exits via the hallway.

### WILL

Do you think he likes me?

### RANDY

I can pretty much guarantee it.

### WILL

Where do you suppose he went?

### RANDY

To the john, I expect.

### WILL

I guess even big Hollywood stars have to take a piss, although they never do in the movies.

### RANDY

Notice that did you? I've gone on long cattle drives without ever once visiting a tree. The horses let loose every now and again, but they edit that out.

### WILL

I can hardly believe I'm here. I wasn't sure Mr. Grant was sincere when he invited me to drop by for a drink. I almost thought maybe the address he gave me was fake. You know, just to get rid of me. But no, here I am. He's so much better looking in person. I mean I get weak in the knees when he looks at me.

## CARY AND RANDY

RANDY

Here's the thing, Will. Some actors are pretty much in real life like the characters they play in movies. You know, guys like John Wayne, Errol Flynn, Jimmy Stewart. But Cary's not really so smooth and sophisticated as you might expect. He's a complicated guy. He had it tough growing up. He's got all the self-confidence of a fat 13-year-old girl with pimples.

WILL

Really? I would never have thought that. What should I do?

RANDY

Be appreciative. He likes that. But don't expect him to ring you up tomorrow for a date.

WILL

I know. I'm not some star-struck fan. I know how these things work. Plus, you're his steady, aren't you?

RANDY

We've been hanging out together since before you were born.

WILL

Really? That long?

RANDY

Not quite. But for a long time.

Cary returns. He has changed into casual, but still elegant clothes.

CARY

Still here, corporal? I thought you might have had a change of heart and fled into the night.

## CARY AND RANDY

					WILL
				(standing up)
We marines don't retreat, sir. Shall I follow you?

Cary puts an arm around his shoulder.

					CARY
This way, soldier. I'll show you a bedroom where Carole Lombard once slept.

					WILL
Really? Who with?

					CARY
Wouldn't you like to know.

As Cary and Will exit via the hallway Cary flashes a smile and waves to Randy, who gives him a thumbs up sign. Randy lights a cigarette, switches on the radio to dance band music, and goes out via the French doors to the patio. He looks up at the moon, then returns, sits in the chair, and snuffs out his cigarette. Randy nods off as the lights dim and the music fades away to silence.

Stage left illuminates, revealing Mrs. Elsie Leach, Cary Grant's 63-year-old mother. She fidgets with her dress and picks out a piece of chocolate from a box on her lap. She takes a bite, makes a face, and returns the rest of it to the box.

					ELSIE
Marzipan. That was nasty.
				(looking about)
They said my son Archie was going to visit, but I suppose he changed his mind. Or forgot. He's about as reliable as his father was.

## CARY AND RANDY

Cary, wearing a silk dressing gown, stumbles into the living room and switches on a lamp. Randy wakes with a start.

RANDY

What? What time is it?

CARY

Shhh, it's late. Hello, Ma. What a nice surprise.

ELSIE

So you say. You sound so far away.

CARY

I'm in California, Ma. That's where you should be too. I worry about you constantly. I know the docks at Bristol are getting bombed.

ELSIE

We should have taken care of those Huns once and for all after that first bloody war. Burned down all their factories. Left them with nothing but a few rusty knives. And barefoot too. It was those Americans and their Mr. Wilson who let them off so easy. I heard somebody else talking there. Who's that with you?

CARY

Randolph Scott. Remember? I told you about him.

ELSIE (distastefully)

Another one of those actors. I might have known.

CARY

How are you feeling, Ma?

## CARY AND RANDY

### ELSIE
I have my aches and pains, but I get by.

### CARY
Are you sure you're OK? You're not just saying that?

### ELSIE
Fat lot you'd care. You didn't lift a finger when your father stuck me in that mental asylum.

### CARY
Dad told me you were dead, Ma. I was just a kid. I had no way of knowing what he did.

### ELSIE
I spent 20 years in that hellish place–just so he could shack up with some woman and run around with his tarts. Sticking me in that snake pit was cheaper than a divorce. He didn't care how much I suffered. You knew he was a cheat and a liar, Archie. You could have made some inquiries.

### CARY
I thought you were dead, Ma! I was only nine years old.

### ELSIE
So you say. And did you ever think to bring some flowers to decorate my grave? Did you ever ask your father where I was supposed to be buried?

### CARY
Of course, I did, Ma. He refused to talk about it. You know how hard he was to talk to. And then I was living over here. I almost never heard from anyone back home.

ELSIE

Never made the effort, you mean. Being a big-shot in the moving pictures and all. And leading a life of dissipation like your father.

CARY

That's not the way it was, Ma.

ELSIE

Oh? And how long were you married to that blond girl before you cast her aside?

CARY

She divorced me, Ma. I tried to make a go of it, but we weren't suited for each other.

ELSIE

It's your life, Archie. You don't have to pretty it up for me. I washed my hands of you a long time ago.

CARY

Aw, Ma, don't be that way.

ELSIE

What a shock when he showed up here after all those years. Him with his flashy suits and posh accent and fancy manners. I thought he was an imposter, I did. Like maybe he'd done in my real son and stole his identity. I'm still not totally convinced that man is my Archie.

CARY

How can you say that, Mother? I'm your son all right. Aren't you proud that I made good?

## CARY AND RANDY

### ELSIE

I suppose. If you say so.

### CARY

If you'd come to America, Ma, I'd make it up to you. I'd take care of you. You'd like it here.

### ELSIE

I'm not going anywhere. Not at my age. I told you that already. You just want me to get torpedoed by some U-boat so I'm out of your hair.

### CARY

Ma, how can you say that?

### ELSIE

You think I want to live someplace where my son associates with the lowest sorts of actors and movie people? Everyone knows what that crowd is like.

### CARY

I'm married to Barbara Hutton now, Ma. I told you that. She's quite respectable. You know, her family owns all those Woolworth's stores. I'm helping her raise her son. He's two and quite the spunky little chap. We're a family now. You could live with us. Or, if you like, I could set you up in your own house. With a maid and someone to do the cooking.

### ELSIE

Oh, you don't like my cooking now is it? Not fancy enough for you, I expect. Sorry, Archie. Not interested. Well, I guess you're not taking me for my walk. It looks like rain anyway. Probably be snow and sleet by tea time. And then more German bombs to terrify us in our beds.

## CARY AND RANDY

            CARY
I hope not. Good-bye, Ma. I'll call you soon.

            ELSIE
Don't bother. I can hardly hear you on those overseas trunk calls. Too much static. And God knows who's listening in. Probably Hitler himself.
            (She picks out another piece of
              chocolate and bites into it.)
That's better. Toffee. I like toffee.

Stage left goes dark.

            RANDY
Charming woman, your mum.

            CARY
Isn't she? And that was her in a good mood. You should see when she's not feeling so chipper.

            RANDY
How's your young marine?

            CARY
Snoring away. Sounds like the German Army assaulting the Maginot Line.
            (Taking Randy by the hand.)
Come on, old man. Let's go to bed.

They walk toward the hallway exit.

Blackout.

# ACT I
# Scene 2

Setting: Same scene. The following morning.

At rise: Cary, Randy, and Will are having toast and coffee around the coffee table. The marine is dressed in his uniform, but his hosts are wearing matching silk dressing gowns.

### WILL
So your first picture together was "Hot Saturday"? I guess I never saw that. When did it come out?

### CARY
Way back in 1932. You didn't miss much.

### RANDY
Cary played the rich cad. I played the sincere young man.

### CARY
Typecasting, don't you know.

### WILL
So who got the girl in the end?

### RANDY
I did naturally.

### CARY
Movies are seldom true to life.

### WILL
I thought you were both great in "My Favorite Wife."

## CARY AND RANDY

**RANDY**
Another realistic picture. I spent seven years shipwrecked alone on a remote island with Irene Dunn and supposedly never touched her.

Will and Cary look inquiringly at him.

**RANDY**
Sorry to disappoint you, boys. I'd have made a grab for her. For sure. No way I could pass up Irene Dunn in a grass skirt.

**WILL**
Didn't anyone see the irony in casting you two as rivals for Irene? I mean considering all the years you lived together?

**RANDY**
Sure they saw the irony, Will.

**CARY**
It was the studio's little joke.

**WILL** (to Cary)
And there was that scene where you first saw Mr. Scott on the diving board at the hotel swimming pool. It looked to me like you were way more interested in him than in your long-lost wife.

**CARY**
Well, Randy does look his best in swim trunks.

**RANDY**
Thanks, Cary. I try to keep in shape.

## CARY AND RANDY

**WILL**
Here's another question. Did it annoy you that Joan Fontaine won best actress for "Suspicion" while you got passed over?

**CARY**
Certainly not, Will. Just because that woman has the I.Q. of a small rock and the sex drive of a rabbit, it doesn't follow that I should resent her ill-gotten success.

**WILL**
And how about the "The Philadelphia Story"? Jimmy Stewart got the Oscar, but you weren't even nominated. That seems so unfair.

**CARY**
Always a bridegroom, never a bride. I don't put much stock in those awards. I'd rather win at the box office. That's what counts in this town.

**WILL**
And what about Mae West?

**CARY** (snappish)
All right. What about her?

**RANDY**
He's pretty touchy about Mae West.

Stage left illuminates, revealing sultry Mae West in sequins and diamonds.

**MAE WEST**
Sure I discovered Cary Grant. He was sweeping the floors at Paramount when I spotted him.

## CARY AND RANDY

### CARY

Not true. I had made seven pictures before she showed up. The studio was paying me $750 a week. And that was no small potatoes back in 1932.

### MAE WEST

Peanuts. The man was making peanuts when I yanked him out of the chorus line. I said if that man can talk, I want him as my co-star. I put him in my first picture, "She Done Him Wrong." I cast him as a Salvation Army captain, if you can believe that. Of course, I do like a man in uniform. Our little picture made over $2 million for Paramount, which saved their bacon. Hauled 'em right up out of the Depression. Made their bankers very happy. Made me a bigger star than Shirley Temple, who confidentially is actually a midget in disguise. Got Cary a big raise too, not that he ever showed much gratitude.

### CARY

The woman is as sexy as Wallace Beery in drag.

### MAE WEST

I'll overlook that last remark. Then I cast him in my second picture, "I'm No Angel." The title referred to me, not–alas– to Mr. Grant, who can make a shy boy scout seem like a sex fiend.

### CARY

I didn't want the part, but the studio forced me. They threatened to put me on suspension if I refused.

### MAE WEST

The man didn't recognize a good thing when it slid into his lap. I wrote the script myself for that picture. They paid me an extra hundred grand for that. You can't expect someone with my talent and sex appeal to slave away at a typewriter for free. I played a wronged woman who had to sue Cary for breach of promise. It was realistic too, since I realized that the only way a girl could get that fellow into her bed was by court order.

CARY

Wouldn't work, Mae. I'd pick prison over you.

MAE WEST

You probably would too. Anyway, that picture earned another $2 million for a grateful Paramount. Everyone in the cast came out covered in glory, particularly me. And that, ladies and gentlemen, is how I made a star out of Cary Grant.

CARY

You mean how I made a star out of you! All those people buying tickets were coming to see me!

MAE WEST

The man is an extremely ornamental fool. Notice I'm being charitable. I didn't say eunuch. And if I had it to do all over again, the next time I'd choose Gary Cooper.

Stage left goes dark.

CARY

And stay away, Mae! Poor woman. She's bitter because her career is on the skids. She turned out to be a flash in the pan, while I'm still pulling in the big box-office grosses.

RANDY

She's got a lot to offer, Cary. You should go up and see her sometime.

## CARY AND RANDY

CARY
Sorry, I don't like to stand in long lines. With her it's take a number and wait.

WILL
I read somewhere, Cary, that you thought the head guys at Paramount resented your success in those Mae West pictures.

CARY
I figured out I was never going to be their fair-haired boy. They couldn't deal with Randy and me living together. So I was always their last choice for movie parts: right below W.C. Fields and the Marx brothers. They'd rather cast chubby Bing Crosby in his wig and corset than me.

WILL
That's so stupid that a studio would sabotage their most promising star.

CARY
Stupidity has never been a hindrance to executive success in this town. So, tired of being low man on the totem pole at Paramount, when my contract was up I went down the street to Columbia.

RANDY
That meant he was working for Harry Cohn, Hollywood's supreme ball-breaker.

CARY
Harry looks almost human, but he's actually the product of a gorilla mating with a scorpion.

## CARY AND RANDY

RANDY

More like a cross between a grizzly bear and a junkyard dog.

Stage left illuminates, revealing Harry Cohn smoking a big cigar.

HARRY COHN

Actors! Who needs 'em! I started with nothing and built Columbia Pictures into a major studio. Won the Oscar for best picture with "It happened One Night." That shocked a lot of the big swells in this town. Bounced us off Poverty Row for good. So where did it get me? Every day I got bankers and unions ripping my ass. And don't get me started on actors. Disney has the right idea. He doesn't have to worry about Mickey Mouse and Donald Duck getting busted on a morals charge. And look at Zanuck cleaning up with Rin-Tin-Tin. Perverse, that's what actors are. Hell, I got broads under contract who get more tail than I do. And half the he-men strutting around my lot are always slinking off to suck each other's cock--or worse. Frankly, I don't get the appeal. What with modern science you'd think the studio commissary could put something in the food to put the kabosh on that. No dice. So there's Cary Grant living brazenly with Randolph Scott. I mean both names on the goddam mailbox as bold as brass. It's some bachelor setup they got out there at the beach. Hell, I got to send girls to lounge by their pool every time some fan magazine wants to do a feature on 'em. I'd tell 'em all to drop dead, but you need actors to sell tickets. That's the movie racket for you. Take a memo: We need to find a property to team Rita Hayworth and Cary Grant. That combo sounds like box-office dynamite.

Stage left goes dark.

## CARY AND RANDY

**CARY**
I'm still waiting for that to happen.

**WILL**
Did you see Rita Hayworth in "You Were Never Lovelier?" She really lit up the screen dancing with Fred Astaire.

**CARY**
Yeah, I saw it.

**RANDY**
Cary's better looking than Fred, but nobody's going to buy a ticket to watch Cary Grant sing and dance. More coffee, Will?

**WILL**
Sure, thanks.

Randy refills his cup. They all sip their coffee.

**WILL**
Any plans to enlist, fellas?

**CARY**
We tried. The fools don't want us.

**RANDY**
I was over in France with Pershing in the first war. I lied about my age to enlist. I thought for sure the Army would want me back, but they said no deal.

**CARY**
And he actually knows how to shoot a gun and ride a horse. The British government tells me I can do more for the war effort by making movies over here.

## CARY AND RANDY

RANDY
He also does some cloak and dagger work for them on the side.

WILL
Really, Cary? You're a spy?

CARY
I do my bit for king and country. But keep that under your hat.

WILL
Sure thing. So how did you two meet?

RANDY
Well, we sort of ran into each other on the beach . . .

Momentary blackout; then the stage lights illuminate revealing Cary and Randy strolling toward each other. They have discarded their dressing gowns, and are wearing 1930s swim attire and carrying beach towels. Both have donned sunglasses. They pass each other, then stop and turn around.

CARY
(raising his sunglasses)
Oh, hello.

RANDY
Hello back at you.

CARY
I've seen you before. You were at that party at Howard Hughes's place.

## CARY AND RANDY

> RANDY

Right. You're that limey who was banging away on the piano.

> CARY

You're that tall, standoffish fellow who never came over to join in the fun. Or get introduced.

> RANDY

I was deterred by the crush of females around you.

> CARY

I'm Cary Grant, the actor.

> RANDY

I know. I read about you in a magazine. You used to be Archie Leach.

> CARY

Well, don't hold that against me.

> RANDY

I'll try not to. I'm Randy Scott.

They shake hands.

> CARY

Glad to meet you. I've met a few randy Scots, but not lately.

> RANDY

Sorry to hear that. I do a bit of acting myself.

> CARY

Oh? Have you been in anything I might have seen?

## CARY AND RANDY

RANDY

Not likely. I've done a few shows at the Pasadena Playhouse. Just small parts. Your friend Howard Hughes got me an audition there.

CARY

Howard's got a finger in many pies. And elsewhere too. So did you enjoy the party?

RANDY

It was OK, except for the music. So I'm curious: which gal did you take home? The blonde or the redhead?

CARY

Neither. I went home alone. How about you?

RANDY

Same here.

CARY

Oh? Don't like girls, or are you just shy?

RANDY (smiling)

Well, I'm not particularly shy.

They study each other for a beat.

CARY

My car's over there. We could go get a drink, if you'd like.

RANDY

Sounds fine. I could go for some lunch too.

CARY

I know just the place.

## CARY AND RANDY

They turn and walk toward the sofa.

                    RANDY
So, are you related to the British royal family?

                    CARY
Almost. I have an uncle who cleans their drains.

Cary and Randy put on their dressing gowns and sit back down as Will applauds.

                    WILL
Sounds like it was love at first sight.

                    CARY
Well, he did move in the same week.

                    RANDY
                (with a wink)
But only to save on rent.

                    WILL
Right. Of course. And how much were you making a week?

                    CARY
More than President Hoover. Or so I was told. But then I was having a better year than he was.

                    RANDY
How about you, Will? Got any plans for when the war's over?

                    WILL
I don't know. I kind of like it down in San Diego. I may go back there and try to get a job in radio.

## CARY AND RANDY

#### RANDY
Being an announcer?

#### WILL
Nah, engineer. They always need guys to keep the vacuum tubes humming. That's assuming there's not some Japanese bullet out there with my name on it.

#### RANDY
Well, keep your head down and don't take any unnecessary chances. You don't need to be a hero.

#### WILL
That's what my folks keep telling me.

#### CARY
I'm sure you'll make it back, Will. You'll be older. You'll have experienced more of life. You'll want to settle down and start a family.

#### WILL
Not likely, Cary. I'm not into girls, or haven't you noticed?

#### CARY
You may change your mind. Everyone needs a family.

#### WILL
Aren't you and Mr. Scott each other's family?

Cary and Randy exchange glances.

#### CARY
I'm afraid we don't qualify, Will. A family is a dad, a mum, and the kiddies.

**CARY AND RANDY**

                    WILL

I don't know if I agree with you on that. Seems to me your family are the people you live with. The people who love you.
                    (looks at his watch)
Gee, it's late. I better get going.

                    CARY

Can I give you a lift somewhere?

                    WILL

Thanks, but I'll be OK. I'll grab one of those big red streetcars going downtown. That's where I catch my bus.

Everyone rises.

                    WILL

Well, it sure has been swell meeting you fellas. It almost seems like a dream.

                    RANDY

The pleasure was ours. You take care.

                    CARY

Naturally, Will, you realize that some discretion will be required here.

                    WILL

I know, Mr. Grant. I'll stay mum about last night. You can depend on me. I know how the world works. You've got my word as a marine on that.

                    CARY

Forgive me for even mentioning it. You're a fine young man, Corporal Gradowski.

## CARY AND RANDY

**WILL**
And OK in the sack, I hope.

**CARY**
More than OK. You did wonders for this civilian's morale.

Randy helps Will on with his coat.

**WILL**
The pleasure was mine. Thanks for being so welcoming. I feel like I'm the luckiest soldier in the whole Marine Corps.

Will hugs Cary and then Randy.

**WILL**
Well, I'll be off. You mind if I write to you sometime?

**CARY**
Please do. We'd love to hear from you.

**WILL**
Thanks. Will do.

Will exits via the exterior door.

**RANDY**
Nice kid, huh?

**CARY**
The best. I hope he makes it.

**RANDY**
Yeah, me too.

### CARY AND RANDY

                    CARY
You want to go back to bed, cowboy?

                    RANDY
I've got the time if you've got the itch. That marine didn't wear you out?

                    CARY
He just warmed me up. Bed or bathtub?

                    RANDY
Surprise me.

Cary takes Randy's hand and they exit via the hallway.

Blackout.

Curtain

## ACT II
## Scene 1

Setting: Same scene, late at night a few days later.

At rise: Moonlight streaming in through the French doors provides a dim light. Repeated loud knocking is heard on the exterior door. Cary, in his dressing gown, enters sleepily from the hallway, and switches on the floor lamp. He wraps his robe tighter and edges toward the door.

                    CARY (warily)
Who is it? What do you want?

### CARY AND RANDY

> MAN'S VOICE (gruffly, o.s.)

Police! Open up!

> CARY

Police? No one here called the police.

> MAN'S VOICE (o.s.)

Open up in the name of the law!

> CARY

Oh, Jesus. What the . . .

Cary unlocks the door and two people burst in: Will Gradowski, now dressed in the uniform of a Los Angeles policeman, and Louella Parsons.

> CARY (surprised)

Will, you're back! What's the matter? And Louella Parsons! What are you doing here?

> WILL

The name's not Gradowski. It's Parker. Butch Parker. I'm a detective with the Los Angeles vice squad. And you're under arrest!

> CARY

Under arrest! For what!?

> LOUELLA

You're done for, Cary Grant! I've got the goods on you at last. You're going down on a morals charge. And we're going to make it stick! It's the scoop of a lifetime!
> (laughing diabolically)

This story will make me the queen of the Hollywood press corps!

## CARY AND RANDY

CARY

But, but I haven't done anything!

WILL

Says you, buddy! You seduced a member of the Los Angeles police force!

CARY

But, Will, you're not a cop, you're a marine. And going to bed with me was your idea.

WILL

Now you've insulted our distinguished fighting men. Locking you up will be a real pleasure.

CARY

But, Will. You were so enthusiastic. So adept. So well-equipped.

WILL

I was doing it for the taxpayers of Los Angeles. It was my duty. I found the act morally reprehensible and personally repugnant.

CARY (dubious)

You found making love with Cary Grant repugnant? What jury is going to believe that? Besides, it's your word against mine.

LOUELLA

That's where you're wrong, smart guy! Detective Parker, show him your camera.

Will unbuttons his jacket, revealing a miniature camera strapped to his stomach.

### CARY AND RANDY

                    WILL

I got it all down on film. Enough to send you away for a long, long time. Come along, buddy. I'm taking you downtown.

Will hastily re-buttons his jacket.

                    CARY

Now, wait a minute. Let's talk this over. We can straighten this out. Call Harry Cohn at Columbia Studios. Or Dory Schary at RKO Pictures. I'm sure an accommodation can be reached.

                    LOUELLA

Not going to work this time, Cary. Bribery won't work. Detective Parker here is incorruptible.

                    CARY

Incorruptible? How can that be if he works for the Los Angeles police?

                    WILL (proudly)

I'm the one good apple in the barrel.

Will draws his gun and points it at Cary.

                    WILL

Come along, buddy. Don't make me shoot you for resisting arrest.

                    CARY

Not so fast, flatfoot. I happen to be personal friends with mobster Benny Siegel, better known as Bugsy Siegel, the notorious hit man for Murder Incorporated. One phone call from me and you'll be sightseeing at the bottom of Santa Monica Bay.

WILL

The joke's on you, twinkle toes. It was Bugsy who gave us the tip on your activities. You muscled in on one too many dames at his parties.

CARY (desperate)

Louella! I'll pay you! I'll pay you any amount you name!

LOUELLA

Just a minute, detective. How much do you make a week?

WILL

$73.54, plus uniform allowance.

CARY

That little? That wouldn't even cover my bar tab at Ciro's.

WILL

It's a struggle. I've got five kids too and another on the way.

LOUELLA

Gee, what did you do? Get married when you were 12?

WILL

No, 14. But I was very mature for my age.

Cary and Louella look questioningly at him.

CARY

See, I can solve your problems right now. And, Louella, I know a hard-working journalist like you can always use a

## CARY AND RANDY

modest bonus. I happen to have my checkbook right here in my robe.

Cary takes out a checkbook and fountain pen.

### WILL
You sleep with your checkbook?

### CARY
I do. I find my bank balance comforting. Now, how about I write you out a check for $5,000 and we call it a night? How does that sound? Or I could go up to $10,000 if you insist.

### LOUELLA
Won't do, Cary. Won't do at all. You won't get off that easy. We want $2,412,862.47.

### CARY
$2,412,862.47! My God! That's my exact net worth!

### LOUELLA
Yeah, down to the penny. We're cleaning you out, Cary.

### CARY
But, but you'll leave me penniless! Destitute!

### WILL
It's your choice, buddy. Destitute or disgraced. And wearing prison stripes! You choose. And make it quick. I'm double-parked out there.

### CARY
All right. You win. I guess I don't have any choice.

Cary starts writing the check as Will holsters his weapon.

**CARY AND RANDY**

WILL

Make it out to George "Butch" Parker, L.A.P.D. I'll give Miss Parsons her cut later.

CARY

This, this really is too much, Will. I trusted you. I invited you into my home.

WILL

I told you, buddy. The name's Parker.

Cary tears off the check and hands it to Will.

CARY

There. I hope you blood-sucking extortionists are satisfied.

LOUELLA

Very satisfied, Cary. You've just handed us another piece of evidence to use against you in a court of law.

CARY

What!

WILL

Attempted bribery of a police officer. That's another felony, buddy.

CARY

Give me back that check!

WILL

No way, buster. This is evidence. Evidence for the prosecution! You're going down, buddy. Or should I say up? Up to San Quentin! For a good long stretch!

### CARY AND RANDY

              CARY

Give it to me!

Cary starts chasing Will and Louella around the room.

              CARY

Give it to me! I say give me that check! Right now!

Will and Louella run out the exterior door as Cary tries to pursue, but he is now moving in slow motion. He flails his arms slowly, but can't make any progress toward the door. At that moment Randy, wearing his dressing gown, runs in from the hallway. He grabs Cary and starts shaking him.

              RANDY

Cary! Cary! Wake up!

              CARY

Wha–? What's happening?

              RANDY

You were shouting in your sleep, honey. You must have been having a dream.

              CARY

Not a dream. It was a nightmare! Louella Parsons and a traitorous cop were cleaning out my bank account. Every last cent!

              RANDY

That does sound nasty. Well, come back to bed, pal. It was only a dream.

Randy puts his arm around him and leads him back toward the hallway. On the way Randy closes the exterior door.

### CARY AND RANDY

#### CARY
It was terrifying. They had a camera! A concealed detective camera! It was pointing right at me!

#### RANDY
Yeah. Well, you know what Sigmund Freud would say about that.

Blackout.

# ACT II
## Scene 2

Setting: Evening at the beach house a few months later. Some of the furniture has been taken out and the pictures removed from the walls. Remaining are the piano, bookcase/bar, and console radio. Two wooden folding chairs have been substituted for the sofa and chair.

At rise: Randy is packing books into cardboard boxes. Cary, dressed for mild weather, enters via the exterior door.

#### RANDY
Hey, there's my favorite movie star.

#### CARY
(looking about)
Who? Cesar Romero? Claude Rains? Edward Everett Horton?

#### RANDY
No, Archie Leach.

#### CARY
Oh, him. Damn, Randy! Somebody stole our furniture!

### CARY AND RANDY

RANDY
I told you we're supposed to be cleared out by the end of the month.

Cary goes to the bar and fixes two drinks.

CARY
So you're serious about selling this place?

RANDY
I told you. It's a big expense and we're hardly ever here. I'm mostly at my ranch now. And you're living with Barbara.

CARY
Don't remind me.

RANDY
And I'll be leaving soon on my USO tour.

CARY
Doing what? Some light yodeling and fancy rope tricks? Shooting the stripes off a sergeant at 50 paces?

RANDY
They signed me up to perform some skits with the comic Joe DeRita. I'm the straight man.

CARY
That goes without saying. Joe DeRita, huh? I knew him back in vaudeville when we were kids.

RANDY
He's a very funny guy.

## CARY AND RANDY

> CARY

Sure, but I bet those troops would rather see pretty girls in skimpy costumes.

> RANDY

We may have some of those too.

> CARY

But you'll be back eventually. Even Bob Hope comes home once in a while to change his socks and read his fan mail. We're not hurting for money, Randy. We could keep this place.

> RANDY

I offered to let you buy out my share.

> CARY

I don't want it without you.

Cary hands Randy a drink. They clink glasses.

> RANDY

Here's to better days.

> CARY

I wish.

They pensively sip their drinks.

> RANDY

You want the radio set?

> CARY

No, it's too streamlined for Barbara. She goes for French Provincial. I suppose you're planning to sell my piano too.

## CARY AND RANDY

**RANDY**
I'm hoping to get a bidding war going for it between Jose Iturbi and Oscar Levant.

Cary plays a few notes on the piano. The last note sounds very out of tune.

**CARY**
More likely we'll wind up having the Salvation Army haul it away. Are you going to marry that girl of yours?

**RANDY**
I'm thinking about it.

Cary plays the melody of "The Wedding March."

**CARY**
She's 20 years younger than you are.

**RANDY**
So?

**CARY**
So that would make an age difference of 40 years between your first wife and your second wife. That's four decades! That's longer than I've lived! Hell, when George Gershwin was 40, he'd been dead for a year.

**RANDY**
Your point being?

**CARY**
Oh, nothing. Just pointing out the peculiarities of your love life.

## CARY AND RANDY

                    RANDY
Some might say you're the biggest peculiarity in that department.

                    CARY
No. I'm the one who makes sense.

Cary starts looking through the mail in the basket on top of the piano.

                    RANDY
You want these old scripts of yours?

                    CARY
Of course. Someday I'll be donate them to a prestigious library and claim a big tax deduction.

                    RANDY
That's what I like about you, Cary. You're always figuring the angles.

                    CARY
I learned it from you. If the income tax goes any higher, I may be deducting my balls, pickled in a jar of formaldehyde and shipped off to Uncle Sam.

Cary starts reading a letter, and sits on one of the wooden chairs.

                    RANDY
You'll have to go through the records and pick out the ones you want. I'm claiming all the Tommy Dorseys.

Cary doesn't reply.

## CARY AND RANDY

**RANDY**

Something the matter?

**CARY**

It's that young marine we befriended a few months back. I got a letter from his friend Ken. Corporal Gradowski didn't make it. He was killed on Guadalcanal.

**RANDY**

Damn, that's awful.

**CARY**

They were attacking fortified positions, and he was hit by mortar fire. The medics evacuated him alive, but he died the next day.

**RANDY**

I'm sure sorry to hear that. He was a nice kid.

**CARY**

The best.

Cary turns over the letter and reads the back.

**CARY**
(handing letter to Randy)

Here, Randy. Read the P.S. on the back.

**RANDY**
(reading aloud)

P.S. Will carried in his pack a framed photo of you and Irene Dunn from the movie "Penny Serenade." His buddies in his unit always kidded him for being sweet on such a mature, older lady. They didn't think Miss Dunn compared as a pin-up to the likes of Betty Grable or Rita Hayworth.

## CARY AND RANDY

Randy hands the letter back to Cary.

RANDY
That's sweet.

CARY
I should show this letter to Irene.

RANDY
I don't think that's really the point he's making.

CARY
I know. But she might appreciate the compliment anyway.

RANDY
I hope he didn't suffer.

CARY
I know. That would have been terrible for him.

Stage left illuminates and we see Will Gradowski in his marine uniform.

WILL
The morphine numbed the pain, but couldn't do much for the panic and terror. The doctors did their best, but I knew I was done for. Nobody could survive my wounds. Too much of me was blown apart and burned. It's scary lying there knowing you're going to die. Especially when you've hardly started living. But I guess that's what war's all about: killing off the young men until one side gives up.

CARY
We're so sorry, Will.

### CARY AND RANDY

**WILL**
That's OK, Cary. I drew the short straw. My time was up. You can't change fate. I've got some good news for you.

**CARY**
What's that?

**WILL**
You're going to be nominated for another Academy Award next year.

**CARY**
Oh?

**WILL**
But you're going to lose this time to Bing Crosby.

**CARY**
Bing Crosby! Are you sure about that? He's fatter than I am. Paramount has to cinch him into a girdle and tape his ears back. He wears a toupee that required more engineering than a B-29.

**WILL**
It's in the cards, Cary. He plays a priest. You can't compete with God.

**CARY**
I suppose not. Now I'm glad his house burned down. So I'll never win an Oscar?

**WILL**
You won't win one, but you'll receive one.

## CARY AND RANDY

**CARY**
I didn't know they did that.

**WILL**
Only for very special people.

**RANDY**
How's Cary's marriage to Barbara Hutton going to work out?

**WILL**
Not so good. They'll have some breakups and reconciliations, but get divorced in the end.

**CARY**
Damn! I may not be cut out for marriage.

**WILL**
Well, you'll try it three more times.

**CARY**
What!

**WILL**
That's right. You'll be married five times.

**CARY**
And will any of them be happier than my first two?

**WILL**
Some of them. Things will get better. You'll work hard on your personal problems. You'll overcome your childhood demons, and manage to forgive your father and mother. You'll achieve a measure of peace and serenity. You'll get to

## CARY AND RANDY

like yourself better. And have the family you always wanted.

A photo of Sophia Loren is projected on a scrim above Will.

CARY

My goodness! Is that one of my wives?

WILL

No. It's someone you'll meet on a movie set. You'll fall in love and want to marry her.

CARY

I can see why.

RANDY

So what goes wrong this time?

WILL

She'll love you, Cary. Just as much as you love her. But she'll be looking for security. She'll decide she can't find it with you.

CARY

Why not?

WILL

Well, for one thing, at that time you're already married.

CARY

How inconvenient. But I expect by then I'll know some experienced divorce lawyers.

### CARY AND RANDY

**WILL**
True, but she'll find out you had an affair with someone else on the same movie set.

**CARY**
I never could resist a pretty face.

**WILL**
Or a handsome one, as it turns out.

**CARY**
I see. In other words, I mess it up.

**WILL**
I'm afraid so.

**RANDY**
How about me, Will. Do I marry Pat?

**WILL**
You do. And you'll stay married until you die.

**RANDY**
I hope that's for a long time.

**WILL**
It is. For a very long time.

**CARY**
And are they happy?

**WILL**
That's hard to say. Mr. Scott is the enigma here. His heart is buried very deep.

## CARY AND RANDY

CARY

I know. I've been digging for it for a decade and have yet to discover any signs of it.

RANDY

Hey, that's not true.

WILL

Well, I've got to go. Kenny's ship is going to be torpedoed tonight, and I want to be there to meet him.

CARY

Sorry to hear that. Well, thanks for all the insights you've given us.

WILL

That's just the thing, fellas. I'm not really supposed to be here. I'm sorry: when I'm gone you won't remember a thing. Well, so long. Thanks again for giving me that special day . . . and night.

The photo of Sophia Loren fades away as stage left goes dark.

CARY

What was that?

RANDY

Just the crashing of the surf. It's a wild night out there.

CARY

I need another drink. How about you?

RANDY

No. I'm still working on this one.

## CARY AND RANDY

Cary goes to the bar and freshens his drink.

### CARY
I feel bad about selling this house, Randy. Be honest. Is this the big brush-off? Is that what you're doing here?

### RANDY
Not at all, pal.

### CARY
Are you sure? I feel like this is the end of us.

### RANDY
Aw, it doesn't have to be. We'll still see each other sometimes.

### CARY
I wonder. In my entire life you're the only connection with another human being that's lasted.

### RANDY
You've got plenty of friends, Cary.

### CARY
I'm not talking about friendship. Here's something I've always wondered about. You came from a well-to-do family in North Carolina.

### RANDY
Yeah, Charlotte.

### CARY
You have a loving mother and father. You have siblings you like. You went to good schools and graduated from college. You were regarded as an outstanding young man in your

## CARY AND RANDY

community. You had all these connections back east. So why did you chuck it all and move here?

CARY

RANDY

Why? I don't know. I suppose I didn't feel I could live my life the way I wanted to back there.

CARY

Almost every aspect of your life is the opposite of mine. I was an only child. My parents should have been arrested for child neglect. My grandmother qualified as a sadist. The things she used to do to me. I got kicked out of school at age 14. I lived the life of a gypsy with a troupe of acrobats. Yet somehow we connected. Here we are the two of us together in this one particular house that you're about to sell.

RANDY

You know why we have to sell it, Cary.

CARY

Do I? Remind me again.

RANDY

We have a good thing going. We're very lucky. We get to act in movies. It's a cushy job, Cary. We go to the set and work with interesting and creative people. We go to restaurants and always get a prime table. We take someone dancing and columnists write about it in newspapers. Every time we turn around a flashbulb goes off in our face. Strangers ask us for our autographs. And every week they hand us paychecks that frankly astound me.

CARY

That's all true.

## CARY AND RANDY

#### RANDY

Hell, Cary, I don't want to give it up. I can't go be an interior decorator like Billy Haines. It's no secret why they drummed him out of the movies. And he used to be one of the top stars at Metro.

#### CARY

So it's the money then. That's what you care about.

#### RANDY

I admit it. Money is important to me. Do you want to go back to selling neckties on the street corner in New York?

#### CARY

That wasn't such a bad racket. Jack Kelly hand-painted the ties. I sold them for $3 each and made $2 profit per tie. On a good day I could clear 30 or 40 dollars, which beats a factory wage. Of course, I had to split my take with Jack.
(wistfully)
Quite a few of my customers would ask for my phone number.

#### RANDY

And what did you say?

#### CARY

I said I was already taken . . . well, most of the time.

#### RANDY

Sounds like you. So you want to go back to doing that?

#### CARY

Of course not. I never want to be poor again. Poverty is wretched. But we can be careful.

## CARY AND RANDY

**RANDY**

We are being careful. By selling this house. And not giving people any more reason to talk. The rumors are circulating, Cary. And getting louder all the time.

**CARY**

And what about love? Where does that figure into your plans?

**RANDY**

You said it yourself, Cary. We're not family. Us as a couple? In public? You have to be kidding. We'd always be the object of derision. Of snickering and gossip. You think people would be standing in line to buy tickets to see our movies? You want to live a life like that?

**CARY**

I don't know what I want. But I know I want you.

**RANDY**

Work on your marriage with Barbara. Try to make a go of it. You know how much you like being a father to her son. Have some more kids of your own.

**CARY**

Barbara drives me nuts every day.

**RANDY**

Then divorce her and find someone else to marry. You can have your pick.

**CARY**

I don't seem to pick very wisely. So you love this new girl of yours?

## CARY AND RANDY

RANDY

We're getting along great.

CARY

That's not really answering my question.

RANDY

Sure, I like her a lot.

CARY

She has money. I suppose that helps with you.

RANDY

Now don't start with the insults, Cary. Sure, I like that Pat has money of her own. I know she's not after me for mine. Isn't that why you married Barbara?

CARY

It was a factor, I suppose.

RANDY

So we're even on that score.

CARY

Not quite even.

RANDY

How's that?

CARY

I loved you. That was the difference.

RANDY

Aw, Cary. Don't be like that.

**CARY AND RANDY**

CARY

So this is where we come to the fork in the trail. You head toward the golden hills with your pretty sweetheart, and I ride off into the sunset with Gabby Hayes.

RANDY

No, I see you more with Andy Devine. You want this book on acting?

CARY

No, you keep it. You need it more than I do.

Blackout.

# ACT II
# Scene 3

Setting: A summer afternoon in 1962, 19 years later. All the furniture has been removed. The room is empty except for a 1950s portable record player on the floor and a few record albums. Some yellowed newspapers are scattered in the corners.

At rise: Cary is out on the patio. The French door is open and we hear the sounds of the surf. He comes in and shuts the door when Randy enters via the exterior door.

CARY

There's my favorite actor.

RANDY
(looking around)
Who? John Wayne? Rock Hudson? Clint Eastwood?

## CARY AND RANDY

CARY
No, you . . . Who's Clint Eastwood?

RANDY
He's that good-looking kid starring as Rowdy Yates in that TV show "Rawhide." Haven't you seen it?

CARY
I never watch westerns.

RANDY
Then I guess you missed the last 20 years of my career.

CARY
I read that your movies were very successful. Congratulations.

RANDY
I hear you're not doing too bad yourself. I caught a matinee of that last picture of yours with Doris Day.

CARY
"That Touch of Mink." How did you like it?

RANDY
You still do the best impersonation of Cary Grant out there. 'Course, I've seen that act before.

CARY
You helped me perfect it.

RANDY
Doris Day, huh? She's been playing skittish virgins about as long as I've been chasing rustlers and shooting horse thieves.

## CARY AND RANDY

**CARY**
Well, she's very good at it. Number one at the box office, you know. Wholesome and adorable. People like that.

**RANDY**
I don't suppose you and her, uh . . .

**CARY**
No.

The men separate and look around the room as they converse.

**RANDY**
I did hear some rumors about you and Grace Kelly.

**CARY**
She's a very charming girl. Rather hard to resist. Inclined to be persistent too. You heard about my latest divorce?

**RANDY**
It's always front-page news. Sorry it didn't work out with you and Betsy.

Stage left illuminates, revealing 39-year-old Betsy Drake.

**BETSY**
I was always a bit mystified why Cary Grant pursued me: Betsy Drake, an obscure actress, hardly a beauty, and 20 years his junior. You'd think a man in his position might be looking for someone more mature, more accomplished. But he persisted and we were married for 13 years–a record for longevity that's not likely to be broken. They sure weren't easy years. Our marriage had more ups and downs than the stock market. As the cliché goes you can't live with him and

you can't live without him. To me marriage involves commitment and that implies monogamy. To Cary a wife is the person you come home to when your latest fling is over. Or not as the case may be. I know the rat was prepared to walk out on me if Sophia Loren had said yes. "Mental cruelty" was the basis of my divorce complaint. Can you blame me?

### CARY

I did love you, Betsy. I never meant to hurt you.

### BETSY

Perhaps not, but that's exactly what you did–many times. One day Cary would be warm and loving. The next day icy and indifferent. You never knew where you stood with the man. True, I'm not that easy to live with either. I have my moods. And I'm not the neatest person; I don't mind a house that looks lived in. Cary Grant is a world-class fussbudget and neat freak. Not an ideal pairing for domestic harmony. Don't get me wrong, I'm not saying I regret our years together. We both helped each other to grow and find ourselves. That has to count for something. I wish we could have made our marriage work, but that was not to be. So now we both have to live with the consequences. And I suspect that's going to be harder for me than for him.

Stage left goes dark. During the following dialogue Cary and Randy circle around and gradually converge in the center of the room.

### CARY

OK, I admit I have my shortcomings. No one looks their best when their character flaws are being dissected in divorce court. How about you, Randy? How are you and your wife getting on?

## CARY AND RANDY

RANDY

Fine. No complaints.

CARY

What's your secret of marital success?

RANDY

Marry the right woman. And treat her with respect. Since I married Pat, I never even kissed another woman. Not even in my movies.

CARY

Really? How do you manage that?

RANDY

I just don't.

CARY

But what if the script calls for it?

RANDY

You forget, Cary, I own the production company that makes my movies. I have full control over the scripts. I may win the girl, but all she gets from me is a friendly handshake. She gets as much affection from me as my horse.

CARY

Very commendable restraint. Though I don't suppose people go to westerns expecting to see a lot of smooching. Sheriff Dillon on "Gunsmoke" never kisses anyone either.

RANDY (surprised)

You watch that show?

## CARY AND RANDY

CARY
Never. . . I see your first wife, that wealthy horsewoman old enough to be your mother, has published her memoirs.

RANDY
Yeah, and sold quite a few books.

CARY
Naturally, I had to send out immediately for a copy. What a disappointment. She didn't even mention you. Not once.

RANDY
I told you, we're friends. Friends don't kiss and tell. You should be happy she didn't rake you over the coals.

CARY
Me? I barely knew the woman.

RANDY
You were never very friendly when she phoned.

CARY
She didn't make much of an effort to conceal her disapproval of me. I could always sense she wanted to take a horsewhip to my hide.

They pass each other and look away.

RANDY
Kind of a shock about Marilyn Monroe, huh?

CARY
Well, she always seemed pretty troubled. We were in that picture "Monkey Business" way back when she was just

## CARY AND RANDY

getting started. She impressed me as just another blonde. Nothing special. Shows what I know.

RANDY

You think it was suicide?

CARY

I only know what I read in the papers. Benny Siegel might have had the inside scoop, but he got whacked back in '47.

RANDY

Howard Hughes doesn't know anything about it?

CARY

Not that he's telling me. My condolences.

RANDY

For what?

CARY

I heard on the morning news that the old cowboy actor Hoot Gibson died.

RANDY

Yep. I heard that too. We're all headed for that last roundup. So the old place is for sale again?

CARY

I thought you might like to look around one last time.

RANDY

Are you thinking of buying it?

CARY

I don't know. You want to go in on it with me?

## CARY AND RANDY

>           RANDY

Looks pretty run down. Take some serious money to fix up this place. And you never know when a big storm could roar in and wipe it off the sand.

>           CARY

Not many big storms make it this far up the coast.

>           RANDY

You'd have to worry about tidal waves too. A major quake could set one off. I thought you were living up in the hills in Howard's old place.

>           CARY

I am. I can look down and see your house over by the country club.

>           RANDY

I'll have to watch and see if I spot any binoculars pointing my way.

>           CARY

I keep my telescope well concealed. How are your investments doing? I hear you have more money than Bob Hope.

>           RANDY

Could be. But probably not as big a pile as you. I guess neither of us has to worry about standing in line at the unemployment office.

>           CARY

I liked your new picture with Joel McCrea: "Ride the High Country."

## CARY AND RANDY

#### RANDY

Thanks. I thought you didn't see westerns.

#### CARY

I made an exception for that one. You know how much I like Joel McCrea.

#### RANDY

He says you were very helpful to his career. You'd turn down a part, so then they'd call him.

#### CARY

Glad to oblige. I'm a bit disappointed you didn't offer that part to me.

#### RANDY

Cary Grant in a western? Doesn't sound right to me. Anyway, I doubt we could have afforded you.

#### CARY

I'd have done it for scale, or close to it. Well, keep me in mind for your next one.

#### RANDY

Won't be a next one. I'm hanging up my movie spurs.

#### CARY

Really? Why?

#### RANDY

I don't think I can top this last one. Might as well go out on a high note. Besides, all that movie-making interferes with my golf game. You thinking of retiring?

## CARY AND RANDY

**CARY**
I tried it about 10 years ago. I got bored.

**RANDY**
Well, you don't look your age. You can still chase those cuties without coming across as a dirty old man.

**CARY**
For a few more years perhaps.

**RANDY**
Who you chasing in your next picture?

**CARY**
Audrey Hepburn. But I'm making her chase me.

**RANDY**
Probably a good idea. Gary Cooper looked pretty silly romancing her in that movie a few years back. What was it called?

**CARY**
"Lust in the afternoon." Or was it "Love in the Afternoon?"

**RANDY**
They should have called it "Love in the Afternoon with Grandpa."

**CARY**
You and I both had long careers. So how come we don't get respect like those new guys Marlon Brando and Montgomery Clift?

**RANDY**
Our mistake, Cary. We tried to act natural. We made act-

## CARY AND RANDY

ing look easy. Those guys are smart. They make acting look hard. You need to sweat more and chew up the scenery.

CARY

Sorry. Not my style.

RANDY

So how's your health?

CARY

Fine. Betsy hypnotized me and got me to quit smoking. I cut down on my drinking too.

RANDY

You still walk around on your hands at parties?

CARY

I don't go to many parties. How about you?

RANDY

In bed by nine most nights. I like to get to the golf course bright and early.

CARY

Still drinking your one beer a day?

RANDY

Always. You could set your watch by it.

CARY

You're a very reliable fellow.

They drift toward each other in the middle of the room and embrace.

## CARY AND RANDY

CARY

You smell the same.

RANDY

You don't. No tobacco smell any more.

Cary tries to kiss him, but Randy turns away. They unclinch and look at each other awkwardly.

CARY

I think about you every day, you know.

RANDY

Same here, partner.

CARY

How come we never see each other?

RANDY

I don't know. Somebody has to make the call.

CARY

I feel awkward phoning your house or your office. I don't know who will answer. You could call me.

RANDY

OK. Where could we go that we wouldn't be seen?

CARY

You could come to my house. Hell, we could go to a restaurant some time. Sharing a meal's not a scandal.

RANDY

OK. Fine by me.

## CARY AND RANDY

CARY

I'm not as messed up as I used to be. Betsy talked me into seeing a therapist. I've been working on my hang-ups.

RANDY

Yeah, I read about you and all those LSD trips.

CARY

I did them under medical supervision. It's an extraordinary tool for connecting to your inner self and getting in touch with your demons. It helped. It really did.

RANDY

Glad to hear it.

CARY

So you don't want to buy this house and live at the beach? Get Bachelor Hall hopping again?

RANDY

Sorry, Cary. I don't look so hot now in a bathing suit. I'm not that skinny kid any more. Besides, every time I open the paper I read about you dating some new starlet or beauty queen.

CARY

You know me, Randy. I see someone attractive and I can't pass them by.

RANDY

Just like our old pal Howard Hughes. And where did it get him?

CARY

It seems to me it got him in bed with plenty of sexy people.

## CARY AND RANDY

**RANDY**
Yeah, and then he went quietly nuts.

Stage left illuminates, revealing a contemporary gum-chewing female movie-goer.

**FILM FAN**
Oh my God! It's Cary Grant!!!

**CARY**
That's right. And who are you?

**FILM FAN**
I'm a film fan from the year [current year]. Wow, it's like so amazing seeing you, considering you died before I was born.

**CARY**
Sorry to hear that. I can only hope you are very, very young.

**FILM FAN**
Who's that old dude with you?

**CARY**
This is Randolph Scott, the distinguished actor.

**FILM FAN**
I thought maybe he was your butler or chauffeur. Oh, Randolph Scott–I remember him now! I never saw any of his movies, but there's some speculation that he was like your BF or something. Like way back in the old days before my grannie was born.

## CARY AND RANDY

RANDY

BF? What's that?

FILM FAN

Boyfriend. You know, your main squeeze. Your families all deny it. They say you were just roommates. Although 12 years seems like a long time for that sort of arrangement. I expect you dudes were always sneaking across the hall and slipping between the sheets. Having a gay old time away from the cameras and bright lights.

RANDY

Not at all. We were just roommates. Saved some big bucks on rent.

CARY

Absolutely. I'm strictly interested in women.

RANDY

The more the merrier in his case. But not Doris Day.

FILM FAN

Hey, guys, it's no big deal these days. I mean, gay people can get married now in every state.

CARY

They've been doing that for centuries.

FILM FAN

No, I mean now they can marry each other. Like totally legally. Guys can marry guys, chicks can marry chicks. Any combo is OK. They have real weddings in churches with ministers and flowers and all the trimmings. My cousin Frankie wound up marrying his tax accountant.

## CARY AND RANDY

                    RANDY
You're joking, of course.

                    FILM FAN
Not at all. They bonded while he was being audited by the I.R.S.

Cary and Randy exchange glances as they consider this.

                    CARY
But isn't it a shocking scandal when homosexuals do that? Aren't they ostracized and ridiculed?

                    RANDY
Don't they risk being fired from their jobs?

                    FILM FAN
Nah, most people are like totally cool with it. It's no big deal these days. A few teachers have been fired who worked for uptight religious schools. The Pope's pretty irate about it as usual. Any time a hurricane blows through, some nut blames it on gay marriage.

                    CARY
Certainly there can't be any actors who've done that. I mean, major actors.

                    FILM FAN
Sure there are. You'd be surprised. So like be honest, were you two ever getting it on?

                    CARY
Certainly not.

## CARY AND RANDY

RANDY

We're just friends.

FILM FAN

OK, if you say so. Wow, I can't believe I'm seeing the late Cary Grant in person. It's like totally blowing my mind. I'm at a party and I've been drinking strange cocktails and gulping down everything people hand me.

RANDY

Was any of it LSD?

FILM FAN

Gosh, who knows? Could be. Damn, I don't feel so hot. I think I'm gonna go throw up.

Stage left goes dark as Film Fan lurches away.

CARY

I wish she hadn't left so soon. I was going to ask her if I was still famous.

RANDY

Sounds like you were. I guess they're still playing your old movies.

CARY

And your movies too, I'm sure. That girl just may not appreciate westerns. What do you think of that men-marrying-men business?

RANDY

Seems kind of hard to believe. A gal in her state may not be totally credible.

## CARY AND RANDY

CARY
Yes, it all seemed rather far-fetched.

RANDY
Exactly. Well, I better be going.

CARY
So soon? Don't you want to check out the rest of the house?

RANDY
I've seen it. I used to live here, remember?

CARY
How could I forget? We were happy here. You have to admit that. We could try it again.

RANDY
I don't get it. Why would you want to shack up with some old fart like me?

CARY
Because 30 years is a long time to love someone. Now I never see you. Not for years and years.
         (making up his mind)
And for that I think you owe me an explanation.

RANDY (gruffly)
What's to explain, pal? You say you love me. So where do I stand in that long line?

CARY
Right at the front. You always have.

## CARY AND RANDY

**RANDY**

We had our shot, Cary. It didn't work out. The Cary Grant Limited is a splendid train that makes many local stops. I was just one of the stations along the way.

**CARY**

That's not true. We could start over again.

**RANDY**

My wife loves me, Cary. I would never do anything to hurt her. Never. We've got responsibilities now. What you're proposing is unthinkable.

**CARY**

You don't think I'm sincere?

**RANDY**

Exactly. I think you're upset from your divorce. And who can blame you for that? You should get married again, Cary. And have a kid. Hell, have a bunch of them.

**CARY**

That's always your solution to my problems. I'm a three-time loser in that department.

**RANDY**

You're young enough to try again.

**CARY**

I'll be 60 in a couple of years. That's pretty old for fatherhood.

**RANDY**

Tell that to Charlie Chaplin. Well, I better go.

## CARY AND RANDY

**CARY**

Look, someone left this record player. Shall we play a song or two for old time's sake?

**RANDY**

OK, but I need to leave soon. I hate getting stuck in rush-hour traffic. Remember this town when the streets were uncrowded and the air was crystal clear? Wilshire was lined with bean fields and you could see the mountains every day of the year.

**CARY**

I was just a 19-year-old kid when I came here for the first time in 1923. Sunshine and movie stars. And that blue ocean right down the road. I knew this was the place for me.

**RANDY**

I felt the same way.

**CARY**

Just one song then. I won't keep you.

Cary puts a record on the turntable and starts it. The tune is "I'm Getting Sentimental Over You" by Tommy Dorsey.

**RANDY**

That's nice. I was worried it would be something by Elvis or Chubby Checker.

**CARY**

Not likely. Care to dance?

**RANDY**

Sure. Why not?

## CARY AND RANDY

They embrace and dance to the slow song. When it finishes, Cary switches off the machine.

### RANDY
Well, it was great seeing you, Cary.

### CARY
You too, Randy. So you'll call me?

### RANDY
I will soon. And don't buy this house, Archie. It wouldn't be a good investment.

### CARY
Yeah. I think I'll take your advice. Thanks for coming.

### RANDY
My pleasure. You take care of yourself.

### CARY
You too.

Randy exits through the exterior door. Projected on the scrim at stage left are a series of famous publicity stills from the early 1930s of Cary Grant and Randolph Scott sharing domestic chores in their home.

Cary unplugs the record player and winds up the cord. He collects the records and picks up the record player. He looks around the room one last time, then exits through the exterior door.

Curtain.

www.ingramcontent.com/pod-product-compliance
Lightning Source LLC
Chambersburg PA
CBHW022107040426
42451CB00007B/167